TWO WORLDS EXIST:
POEMS BY YEHOSHUA NOVEMBER

With all the blessings,

Yehoshua
November

PRAISE FOR *TWO WORLDS EXIST*

"These poems are like a documentary film—close to life, narrating episodes from everyday life (many of them happening within the Chassidic community). But under the skin of these poems a flame of passion—or compassion—is hidden. Hidden and palpable at the same time. That's how Yehoshua November creates such beautiful surprises for his readers."

-Adam Zagajewski

"I have read these beautiful poems many times over. Each time I find something new and wonderful and deeper and more spiritual therein. *Two Worlds Exist* is an even stronger book than November's first collection. So full of sorrow and humility and reverence, love and pain and the actual stuff of our lives—the guilt of the small cruelties we inflict; the large cruelties life inflicts; wavering and unwavering faith that there is something greater than ourselves behind it all."

-Liz Rosenberg

"Yehoshua November's poems are deeply felt, carefully crafted, insightful, and moving. While contemporary American literary culture tends to view 'religious' and 'literary' values in opposition, November's poetry brilliantly bridges this divide. He writes with tenderness, understanding, and disarming modesty; at the same time, his characteristic subjects—the challenges posed by married life, child rearing, and suffering, both physical and spiritual—are among the great subjects of literature and life."

-David Caplan

TWO WORLDS EXIST

ORISON
BOOKS

Two Worlds Exist

Orison Books, Inc.
PO Box 8385
Asheville, NC 28814
www.orisonbooks.com

ISBN- 978-0-9906917-9-2

Distributed to the trade by Itasca Books
1 (800) 901-3480
orders@itascabooks.com
www.itascabooks.com

Manufactured in the U.S.A.

Cover art: "The Carousel" copyright © 2016 by Michael Gleizer. Used by permission of the artist.

ORISON
BOOKS

CONTENTS

IV.

V.

ACKNOWLEDGMENTS

Grateful acknowledgment is made to the publications in which versions of the following poems first appeared:

Cider Press Review: "Conjoined Twins"

Jewish Learning Institute website: "Long Prayer"

Kerem: "Prayer"

Lips: "So Many Poems" and "2AM, and the Rabbinical Students Stand in Their Bathrobes"

Moment Magazine: "One of the Few Jews"

Paterson Literary Review: "Briefly," "From Another World," "Lesson from My Father," "Once, Stopped at a Light Along Rt. 27," "On the Eve of Our Wedding, I Accompany My Father to His Parents' Resting Place," "The Bike," and "The Intended Destination"

Poetica: "In the Middle of the In-Class Essay Exam"

Salamander: "I Made a Decision," "Live Like the Ark in the Holy of Holies," "The Life of Body and Soul," and "The Recently Divorced Adjunct Professor Waits in the High School Chemistry Classroom"

Seminary Ridge Review: "A Young Mother Will Pause, Mid-Song" and "Self-Portrait"

The Sun Magazine: "At the Request of the Organization for Jewish Prisoners," "Between Lifetimes," and "The Soul in a Body"

Virginia Quarterly Review: "Contemporary Poets," "Falling from the Sky," "Two Worlds Exist," and "You Stood Beneath a Streetlight Waving Goodbye"

Zeek: "The Lower Realm"

"Conjoined Twins" was selected as the winner of the London School of Jewish Studies Poetry Contest. "I Made a Decision" and "The Intended Destination" were nominated for the Pushcart Prize. "In the Middle of the In-Class Essay Exam" was a finalist for the Anna Davidson Rosenberg Award for Poems on the Jewish Experience.

———

I would like to thank Miriam Grossman, Maria Gillan, Kurt Spellmeyer, and the Slonims for their encouragement and support. I am grateful to Liz Rosenberg, Rivky Slonim, Gary and Sharon Ickowicz, and Baruch November for their important input on these poems. Special thanks to David Caplan, who selflessly offered his time and wisdom throughout each stage of this book's development. Deepest gratitude to everyone at Orison Books. Fortunate is the author whose work is ushered into print under the care, vision, and editorial expertise of Luke Hankins. Thank you to my family—the Novembers and Reiches—for their continuous support and assistance. Thank you to my children—each one unique, each one with so much to offer to the world. And deepest thanks of all to my wife, Ahuva, whose calm radiance is the foundation of our home.

In memory of Ruthie Baer
(Chaya Rissel Bas Yeshaiya A'H)

TWO WORLDS EXIST

I.

If I wear an ice suit, I can fly beneath the sunset
and not burn, my son said
from the back of the van, as we drove over the bridge
beneath the pink sky.
And if I wear an ice suit, I thought,
perhaps I will finish my days without roasting
in the oven of what one human does to another
or the furnace of what God does to man.

Once, in shul, I sat across from a rabbi
who spoke of his suffering. He said,
I don't have feet to stand on to complain,
but I remember standing in a room, thirty years
ago, the Rebbe raising his voice
to call God to task.

A week earlier, at the ritual bath,
the rabbi realized he had forgotten
his white Sabbath shirt.
In the sanctuary, I watched him stand up
to pray the Silent Prayer
in his undershirt and long black coat.
What role do these moments of minor embarrassment play
in a life of greater miseries?
Could the rabbi concentrate on his prayers?
And if so, what did he ask God for
at that moment?

II.

If I had worn a cage of ice around my heart,
it would not have cracked
as I stood in the cheder's narrow hallway
and heard the principal's matter-of-fact voice say,
concerning one of my children,
We cannot help her.

If I wear a band of silence around my head,
I will hear nothing,

what my youngest daughter hears.
I would like to rise up
and lodge a complaint before God,
but each morning I wake late for prayers
and rush to catch up with the other worshipers.

Once, my wife turned to me and asked,
Do you think this happened because God wanted
to show us what innocence looks like?
Isn't she happier than the others?
Then she turned her face back to her closet
and cried into her blouses.

III.

Two worlds exist:
The higher hidden one
and our earthly realm.
Everything that occurs in this life
flows down from the hidden world.
That which appears good
descends through an infinite series
of contractions until it fits
within the finite vessels of this world.
That which appears tragic
slides down, unmitigated,
from the hidden realm—
a higher, unlimited good
this world cannot hold.
So the mystics explain suffering
if all comes from above,
from where no evil descends.

Is this something one tells another
who is suffering?

This is something one does not speak
but tries to believe
when life no longer seems possible.

When I was younger,
I believed the mystical teachings
could erase sorrow. The mystical teachings
do not erase sorrow.

They say, here is your life.
What will you do with it?

I

A YOUNG MOTHER WILL PAUSE, MID-SONG

A breeze will move the curtain
in a window above a crib.
A young mother will pause, mid-song,
suddenly realizing
the infant she sings to
cannot hear—has never heard—
her voice.

——

I remember driving home from the doctor
with the results of the hearing test,
you recently said.
The white envelope occupying
the empty passenger seat,
like an undesired verdict resting on a court table.

——

I held her on my shoulders
in the apartment parking lot where our neighbors
had gathered for a communal celebration
on the festival of Sukkos:
Live music, dancing, skits.
A friend turned toward me
to trace the source of the feedback
echoing from her new, high-powered hearing aids—
realized the origin, then looked away.

——

With which faces did we greet each other
in our apartment hallway
those months of prayers and waiting rooms,
hoping beyond logic the next expert
could unlock the mystery—
the other kids at home, once more,
with a babysitter,
outmatched by the evening's homework.

——

Once, I found the year's notebook of poems,
written in my few spare moments between two jobs,
cut to pieces under her bed.
From the bathroom, I heard the loud buzz
of an electric toothbrush
she didn't realize she'd left running.

———

I was pulling out of the university parking lot,
the Eve of Yom Kippur,
when you called from the audiologist
to share the news:
The second cochlear implant is working.
She was able to hear my voice.

———

Not working, Mommy,
she says, when she cannot fly
despite the Purim butterfly costume
my wife bought for her at K-Mart.

———

Today, I walked into an empty library.
On a table, a book opened to a page
on hearing loss—
no trace of the one
who'd been reading—
like a love note left by a stranger
for someone else who shares your name.

LESSON FROM MY FATHER

I am just a person who,
because of his Chassidic beard,
appears to have great faith.
Though I look like a rabbi,
in my mind, I am always
the least religious boy in the class,
the son of a doctor in a class of rabbis' sons
who make this distinction clear.

It is early in the morning,
and I am crying in my bed before school.
My father walks in after a night on call,
sits down beside me, and says,
You are you because of you,
not because of me.

CONJOINED TWINS

My father was a resident in the hospital
when my young mother gave birth to them. Two bodies
and one heart.

And hearing that the pathologists at that teaching institution
were coming to learn the lessons
science's rare cases could teach,
my father turned the combination
on his locker and concealed the stillborn baby boys in a box.

Early the next morning, another Jewish resident
stood over the bodies with my father,
performed the ritual circumcisions in the silence
of an unoccupied delivery room.
"Choose names you would not otherwise use,"
the rabbi had instructed over the phone.

At the burial my father asked why
this had happened. "Perhaps you are not
as religious as you should be," the rabbi answered.
And the answer plunged God
into concealment for my father.

"I looked quickly
and saw them embracing,"
my mother later said
of the two boys, who were to be born
between Purim and Passover.

One was named Mordechai,
who gathered all the Jews
when they thought they had been forsaken.
And one was named Pesach,
the holiday when all Jews,
even idol worshippers,
were freed,
as long as they desired to go.

And they left their bondage
and arrived at the mountain
where, the Midrash states,

they camped in the desert
like one man
with one heart.

FALLING FROM THE SKY

When we found out our daughter had gone deaf,
I did not question God's fairness—
not out of faith
but because
my whole life
it had always seemed
that at the next moment
terrible news would fall from the sky—
as punishment, perhaps, for a particular transgression
but more likely
because
whatever you think could never happen—
must happen.
And in this way,
you know clearly
there is a world you do not see.

ON THE EVE OF OUR WEDDING, I ACCOMPANY MY FATHER TO HIS PARENTS' RESTING PLACE

Pink sky slides over grassy plots
and gravel lanes. I try to imagine
what he must be remembering
as he rests his head on the cool rock
of his mother's gravestone:
The house on Lenox Road.
Potatoes for dinner again
beneath the peeling kitchen ceiling.
Her warm voice telling stories about ancestors
bundled against the Russian winter.
Then he and his three sisters
lying down in their coats,
the house's heat turned low
despite the cold Brooklyn night.
Her preparing a lesson plan
beneath a dim lamp in the bedroom,
her husband snoring over on the bed
after losing his job
in one factory or another.

Before our wedding ceremony,
one of the three sisters says,
in the name of her mother,
Marriage is not
fifty-fifty.
Some days it's eighty-twenty,
and some days
it's zero-one hundred.

A drop of rain slid down
the dining-room wall
during last night's dinner.

You cried again after yesterday's meeting
at the kids' school—
another conversation at the kitchen window
overlooking the backyard alders,
gazing through the openings
between the branches.

THE BIKE

You need to get out more,
to exercise and get fresh air,
the doctors told my cousin
after his son drowned
in a terrible accident.
So he started biking wherever he had to go,
but it didn't help.

When I visited his city,
he rode his bike to my hotel.
Later, I watched him turn the corner
and wave goodbye.
I watched until I could no longer see his form—
beard, black pants, white shirt—
bent forward, peddling
his son's old bike
into the long summer evening.

THE INTENDED DESTINATION

Once, at sundown, I drove past the airport
on my way to teach at the night college.

A line of planes stood suspended in the air above the highway,
each awaiting its turn to land.

I am a man with four children
to whom I must nearly be a stranger

as my father was to me.
He would drive home after long nights on call,

snow attacking his windshield
as he made his way

through Scranton's drab streets,
having ushered another life into the world.

Once, at dawn, turning into the alleyway behind our house,
he fell asleep, and his blue station wagon nearly plummeted

through the air, down to the school yard deep below.
How many hours are spent in states outside of life,

in the waiting? Sometimes, as I ascend
the steps to the night class,

the stairwell bathed in weak fluorescents,
a child's face floats up before me

full of sadness or wonderment. I turn
the handle to the classroom door.

II

2AM, AND THE RABBINICAL STUDENTS STAND IN THEIR BATHROBES

2AM, and the rabbinical students stand in their bathrobes
at the edge of the yeshiva parking lot, watching
the practiced motions of muscular firemen disembarking
from their engine. Soon, it will be determined
the youngest student in the building
pulled the basement alarm
after learning, over the dormitory pay phone,
his parents, back in Baltimore, intend to end
their nineteen year marriage before Passover.
The only one the rabbis have not accounted for
crouches in his closet behind a row of black sports coats.
And because the yeshiva caters to souls
but also bodies,
the early morning mysticism class
on why the Divine Presence cannot dwell
amongst those plagued by sadness
has been cancelled.

AT THE REQUEST OF THE ORGANIZATION FOR
JEWISH PRISONERS

Three bearded rabbinical students in a rented car,
trunk filled with menorah kits and grape-juice bottles,
we pulled away from the all-male yeshiva in New Jersey
and headed west, into the heart of Pennsylvania, to celebrate
Chanukah with the Jewish inmates of Allenwood's many prisons.

In our black hats and coats we entered
the lobby of the medium-security compound
and took our place in the check-in line behind a woman
not dressed at all like the rabbinical-school secretary—
the only other female we had seen in weeks.
What was exposed was exposed, and what wasn't
was so tightly garbed that no questions remained
as to proportions or angles.
She had come to visit an inmate.

"We can't let you past the checkpoint dressed like that,"
the crew-cut officer behind the front desk said
to the woman, probably in her thirties, standing, ashamed now,
beside her two small sons. She had
more sensible clothes in her bag, she said.

While she retreated to the bathroom to change,
a Catholic chaplain led us through a courtyard
framed by barbed wire and watchtowers,
across the icy, vacant basketball blacktop,
and into a small multipurpose room,
where Jewish prisoners,
released for that hour from their errands,
were awaiting our arrival.

The priest looking on with a guard
through a two-way mirror,
we poured the grape juice into paper cups
and told the old story of the Jewish flame lasting longer
than nature's laws could explain.

We told the story of the soul,
which, against its will, descends
into the body's confinements.

And then we tried to explain
the great Chassidic paradox
as our Rebbe had taught it to us—
how, despite its loftiness, the soul was created
only to sanctify the body,
to lift up the lowest realm.

The priest re-entered the room.
"About time to wrap it up, rabbis."
So we set out the tin menorah kits and lit the candles,
and then we were ushered once more across the frozen courtyard
and into a warm van, to be driven to the next facility.

As we pulled out, we could see the woman,
now dressed in a puffy coat and plain winter hat,
packing her two sons into the backseat
of her beat-up sedan.
I imagined her dressing in her bathroom that morning,
applying makeup in the mirror above a sink
spotted with children's toothpaste,

thinking not at all of the sexual act
but of how to give her husband or boyfriend
something to look forward to.

She must have inhaled deeply
and then squeezed her body into the tight black dress.

ONE OF THE FEW JEWS

One of the few Jews on the R&B scene,
he played keyboard for the *Marcels*
of 1961 "Blue Moon" fame
until a voice called him back
to the God of his Forefathers
in the middle of a nightclub solo.

Drifting from job to job,
he taught Algebra in the Jewish day school,
tapping his black loafers beneath the teacher's desk.
And on the Sabbath, he sat in the front of the synagogue
praying the Silent Prayer longer than the other men,
asking forgiveness for his former life on the road.

And because he was a kindhearted man
who pitied the slower students,
his voice would rise, "Obvious to *whom*,"
when the others complained he had reviewed the equation
one too many times. And before holidays,
when only a few students would attend,
he'd pull out a red book he kept in his desk
and read to us the story from the Talmud
of the highway robber who transformed his life
and married a great Sage's sister.

Once, as he turned his back
to leave the school building and walk home,
I slipped the peel of a banana he had just given me
into the opening of his worn leather briefcase.
And because I was in tenth grade and he was my teacher,
the universe of the small rented attic
where he opened his bag to see how his kindness had been repaid
did not exist for me, its absence reinforced
the next day when he said nothing in class.

After I graduated, I heard that he had married
one of two blind twins from his hometown,
who also played the piano.
Then, suddenly, he disappeared without a word.
No one in the community ever heard from him again.

Oh, Mr. Males, can it be
that a soul descends into a body
asked to fulfill a mission it cannot complete?
This world is cruelest to the best people.

Please come back, Mr. Males.
Your wife is silently waiting before the piano in the foyer.
Your seat is empty in the front of the shul,
and you were the only one in the whole synagogue
who knew how to pray.

BRIEFLY

I.

Once, on the Sabbath,
she slipped as we walked along the frozen lake
behind her house. Lifting her up, I bent forward, shyly,
to kiss her on the cheek—
the hesitant peck of a bird.

Don't get upset if I sit with him in science class,
the brown-haired, brown-eyed girl,
who was supposed to be my girlfriend, later said,
standing beneath the exit sign
at the back of the Jewish day school,
the small hairs
above her upper lip illuminated
by sunlight shining through glass doors.

But how could I not
when, from across the lab, I heard
their laughter commingling
throughout Mrs. Z's review sheet
on the sexuality of flowers?

And at lunch, how could I not
feel betrayed
when she played two-person tag
on the baseball field
with a boy from the grade below us?

Naturally, the mansion on the sandy island
we had imagined together each night, over the phone—
only a block and two backyards
stretching between us—
floated up and disintegrated into the air
of that Minnesota suburb.

II.

Whether she understood or was hurt by
the series of jokes I then made in class

concerning the trace of hair
above her upper lip—

mock ads for bleach and wax,
weather reports forecasting follicle growth—
I wasn't really sure.
I did not look into her face. Perhaps, once or twice,
we passed each other awkwardly
in the hallway—

until, one evening, I glanced up
from my homework to see my mother and father
standing at my bedroom door,
just returned from a meeting
with the school board.

Her mother said
she had been crying in her room after school,
refusing to go each morning—
the reason finally revealed
at the therapist they'd forced her to see.

As part of their concession
not to enlist a lawyer,
her parents demanded I apologize
in front of the class without mentioning her name.
That summer, I learned we were moving across the country,
where my father had gotten a new job.

When I think of her, I remember the lines
I rehearsed in my bedroom:
A person can hurt another person
very deeply without realizing it
or intending to do so.
I suppose this is what it means to be insensitive.

I remember standing in front
of my math class,
feeling very young and very old,
saying these words,
looking briefly into her familiar eyes.

THE RECENTLY DIVORCED ADJUNCT PROFESSOR
WAITS IN THE HIGH SCHOOL CHEMISTRY
CLASSROOM

Twilight now, and the night school teacher sits beneath
the great chart of the periodic table in the chemistry classroom
the overcrowded college across the street has rented
and assigned to his section of English Composition.

Tonight, the moments before his lecture
on writing the research paper unfold so slowly
he has almost forgotten the short winter day's demand
for more grading and travel than his body can muster.

He has almost forgotten the blitz of snow that will land
against the classroom's night windows
and then on his windshield the entire drowsy ride home
to his new apartment. Now he believes

he will sit beneath the chart of elements forever,
considering the combination of events that has brought him here—
the way one considers admixtures of acids and gasses.
How many years ago was it, he thinks to himself,

that I sat in a room like this one—
beakers of ancient, glowing liquids, Bunsen Burners
casting shadows of flames on the others' faces?

SUDDENLY

A thousand seagulls rise off the river
behind my classroom.
Facing the back windows,
I watch the birds fly
above my students' heads, which—
turned towards me, or our text,
or their texting—
do not witness the synchronized ascent.
Sometimes, remarkable things happen
inside a classroom
but more often
outside it.

III

I MADE A DECISION

Once, before either of us was twenty,
in the cafeteria, I watched your mouth
enclose itself around a plum.
Because I was young and you were beautiful,
I did not say, *This is just a physical body nourishing itself.*
And I did not say, *Perhaps this is the other half of my soul.*
I made a decision with a young man's body,
and my soul continues to thank me.

LIVE LIKE THE ARK IN THE HOLY OF HOLIES

I.

Live like the Ark in the Holy of Holies,
the Rebbe often said,
Two and a half cubits long,
one and a half cubits wide,
one and a half cubits high,
but, paradoxically, occupying no space in the room.

So a man rises from his dark-haired wife in a rectangular bed
according to a precise clock
to earn paychecks in particular amounts
to pay for the life that unfolds within the boundary lines
assigned to his name on a town map
filed in a metal, municipal drawer—

instructed to believe his livelihood,
whatever honor life affords him,
comes from the One with no body and no form.

II.

A thousand years are to You like a passing yesterday,
or a single night watch, the Psalmist wrote.
You pushed through your mother
into the fluorescence of the world,
rushed down your boyhood block
for a haircut before your wedding,
made love for the first and last time,
beginning as a young couple,
finishing with much older bodies
in a distant city.

III.

You hear the Torah read each week—
fifty times a year over so many years—
it is one long reading.
And the young man reading grows old,
standing his whole life at the bima.

And the soul comes down because
it needs something from the body.

THE LIFE OF BODY AND SOUL

or, on rare inspired days,
the life of soul and then body.
And sometimes, both suffer together,
like a man with a bad foot limping through the airport,
late for a flight to a holy city.
One always wants to climb a ladder
back into the weightless air.
The other pulls down
toward the cinderblocks of the world,
spends long hours squinting through desire's lace.
And Yaakov is the soul, and Aisav is the body.
But once, on a tape of a Chassidic gathering,
after the voices of rabbinical students had stopped singing,
I heard a crackling silence,
and then an old rabbi said, *The soul*
is God's greatest opponent. It wants
always to break free of the body,
leaving the world barren of holiness.
And once, many years earlier,
a barren woman entered
the Sanctuary in Shiloh
and prayed so long and intently for a son
that the high priest who presided there
thought she must be drunk—
going on that way about her desires
with God in the room.
But, in the end, the high priest was wrong.
And the laws of prayer mirror her prayer—
her desire reflecting His desire
for the life of souls in bodies.
And, sometimes, the mystics say, the body's desire
is really the soul calling out from underneath—
Yaakov reaching into the world
with Aisav's hands
for the lot the soul has descended to sanctify.
And always, that ascetic, the soul's high priest,
mistakes the body's desires for nothing more.
So that when, for example, I saw you standing
at the soda machine in college, and my body was awoken,
the high priest of my soul,
having just returned from a year in the Holy Land, said,

This is just a young man's desire
for a young woman with long dark hair.
But in the body's version, there are five Jewish children
and our life together.

BETWEEN LIFETIMES

But love is a rusting machine
you call to have serviced over and over again,
hoping the pieces won't have to be replaced. Again and again,
you apply the grease until the engine inches forward.
Between lifetimes, you say words to your wife
unrelated to phone calls from the kids' school
or the leak dripping into the attic.
In the middle of grading a terrible essay
you remember how much you admire her
and you send her an email from the living room.
And if neither of you has fallen asleep,
you lock the bedroom door.
And in the middle, one of your children knocks
from the other side
of the universe.

SO MANY POEMS

So many poems about your dark hair, your dark body.
Storehouse of my private delights. At this moment,
you drive the kids to school in the next town.
It's almost summer. Classes at the university
have let out. I return the fan to the attic window
where the pine tree's upper branches sway.
For breakfast, I've brought up an apple
and glass of water. Are you on the way home?
Have you stopped off somewhere?
So many poems with you as the centerpiece,
and how infrequently I've imagined
how you see our life together.

PRAYER

Before the Silent Prayer,
some slip the hood of their prayer shawls
over their heads,
so that even among many worshipers
they are alone with God.

Primo Levi wrote about the sadness of
"a cart horse, shut between two shafts
and unable even to look sideways. . ."

Let me be like those pious ones
or that horse,
so that, even amidst a crowd,
no other crosses the threshold
of my dreaming.

YOU STOOD BENEATH A STREETLIGHT WAVING GOODBYE

You stood beneath a streetlight waving goodbye
the night we dropped you off in the city
for our daughter's appointment
with one of the country's top surgeons.
And as we drove away, the other children and I
waved back at you,
until, because of the angle and the distance,
your forms disappeared in the light.

And I remembered how, in college,
I would turn back each evening
as I stepped out of your apartment building.
You would poke your young beautiful face
out the second story window,
your arm cutting the cool night air
as you waved goodbye.

And I would walk backwards
over the frosted grass
until I reached halfway beyond the next building,
where, each time, from that distance,
I watched the streetlamp's light
suddenly consume your dark arm and face.

The mystics say creation begins
as a luminescent point,
a flash of wisdom,
containing all that will be
but in an abstract, potential form.

All those nights,
when we were so young,
when your body became a ray of light,
I could not have imagined
the life that lay ahead of us a decade later.
Two boys and two girls,
one who cannot hear.
All of us in a small apartment.
Each with needs as enormous as mansions.

Sometimes, I am afraid you will wave goodbye
and turn away from our life together,
that a man who can make things easier
has been waiting
ever since the mystic's luminescent flash,
growing ever more real and hungry for you
until one day he will materialize
as you load groceries into the van.

I would like to go back to the young woman
waving at the window to the man walking backwards.
I would like to show her this life,
to say she is free to go,
and to ask her if she will still take me.

IV

THE SOUL IN A BODY

is like an old Russian immigrant
looking out his apartment's only window.
Yes, yes, he says,
the landlord printed my name in block letters
on the lobby directory
decades ago.
All correspondence
has been forwarded to this address.
But I am not from here. I am not
from here at all.

IN A CITY OF MODERN JEWS

Gray light spreads across
Saturday afternoon sky.
Bearded, with a long black coat,
the image of your great grandfather coming toward you?
It is just me,
a human being in this century,
with a wife whom I met in college, drawn to her
thin figure.
I am not your great grandfather, though, sometimes,
I feel God spreading
across the sky, humming beneath the drug stores
and parking lots.

———

Do you think faith is foolish, naïve?
The Chassidic Masters say God Himself
is the source of the theories
that contradict His existence.
God Himself breathes life
into the mouth of the professor
declaring to his students
the Divine does not exist.
He is the force moving
the students' pens
as they record His absence in their notebooks
and write it again on the final exam.

———

Let me state it directly:
I am growing older.
I can no longer think of art
as I did when I was a younger man.

———

Deep within the crib beneath the window,
our youngest daughter breaks
the four AM silence. I lie still as a boulder.
She rises from the bed to nurse the child.

Is sleep more important to me
than helping others? Ah, but if I had more sleep
I could help more. A foolish thought.
Rumpled clothing, headache, weary-eyed.

———

I would like to rise up
in the middle of the life I've lived
until now. Like Abraham
circumcising himself at 99 years old,
as if everything he'd accomplished
had been forgotten.

CONTEMPORARY POETS

Has there ever been a group of agnostics so intent
upon meaning
in every car door shutting
in the cold, each turn
of a leaf as it descends?
Do they believe
more than us, dozing off
in the back of the synagogue?

THE POSSIBILITIES OF LANGUAGE

She was a great writer until she had children,
the famous visiting poet said,
sitting at a gleaming table in the hotel lobby,
a glass of fresh-squeezed orange juice in his hand.
Bringing children into this world
is the wrong thing to do, another professor,
who'd climbed to the top of the mountain, advised
in the middle of a class
on the Concerns of Craft.

A child is infinity,
my rabbi said when we met
in the worn-down yeshiva coat room
after my wife had given birth.
A child is infinity, he repeated,
without explaining.

ONCE, STOPPED AT A LIGHT ALONG RT. 27

Once, stopped at a light along Rt. 27
on my way home from class,
I saw an older man stretch out his hands
over a younger man's forehead:
"…May His countenance shine upon you
and be gracious to you…"
A father bestowing the priestly blessing
on his son beside a Toyota
in a supermarket parking lot
the Eve of Yom Kippur.
"…turn His countenance to you
and grant you peace."
The man lifted his body
into the driver's seat of his sedan.
His son resumed loading groceries
into the back of his minivan. The God of Abraham,
Isaac, and Jacob descending
through the shopping cart's metal grates
and onto the asphalt
of the state highway.

THE LOWER REALM

I.

In a room, a father teaches a page of Talmud to his son.
Outside, soldiers search with candles or flashlights,
or they are not looking at all.
The father hears their boots crunching the leaves, or not.
This story is not one of nostalgia, of a lost world.
It is this century. Some Jews are watching the Super Bowl.
Others sit in the Study Hall and never plan to leave.

II.

This world was created through ten Divine utterances.
There are Ten Commandments.
The Ten Commandments are to be ushered into the world
created by ten utterances.
God desires to be here
more than in the higher worlds,
which are not the purpose of creation. If they were,
He could have stopped with them and not created
this lower realm.

III.

In a room, a father teaches a page of Talmud to his son.
Outside, gentiles from Odessa hold torches.
It is the beginning of a pogrom, or it is a hundred
years later, and these Odessans,
named after their great-grandfathers,
are ushering in the next Olympics.
The beginning is wedged in the end.

IV.

At the Neila hour, Jewish boys—
kidnapped from cheder
and raised in the Tsar's army—
unbutton their shirts.
Revealing their whip marks, they whisper,
We did not forget You, please bless us.
Sandy Koufax, a Jew from Brooklyn

who learned little Torah, will not
play baseball on Yom Kippur.
Sometimes, out of nowhere, the soul
awakens in the middle of the life in the body. And the world
cannot go back to its games in the same way.

AMERICAN CHASSID

What is asked of you, American Chassid
        of the new millennium,
who grew up with Sam Cooke's croon floating
        from your father's expensive speakers in the living room,
the Marx Brothers playing in the background
        behind family dinners,
who spent high school summers in his attic bedroom,
        reading Thomas Hardy and trying to forget the face
of the last young Jewish beauty
        who'd decided she needed more space?

Not a hole cut in a frozen lake in lieu of a ritual bath.
        Not an underground cheder beneath
the communists' noses.
        Not execution by NKVD firing squad
in a 2 AM courtyard, leaving behind a wife
        and children, a legacy,
and a quarter loaf of bread.
        You will never be like the Chassidim
of last-century Russia.

A little joy, a little faith. Not believing the world
        is the way it looks on the surface,
and taking some risks based on this belief.
        Knowing you have not really met God
in hours of prayer and mysticism
        if your neighbor still can't
read the Aleph-Beis. American Chassid,
        hot shower then heated ritual bath.
Kosher sushi and veggie burgers. Open the Chassidic discourse
        and read. Watch a video of your Teacher,
gone almost ten years before you became his follower.
        In a synagogue in Brooklyn,
he waves his arms, encourages the others
        to sing an 18th century song with more force, faster, louder.
He sees the holy composer standing before him.
        Like those Jews in Russia, we see nothing.

FROM ANOTHER WORLD

This morning, my seven year old daughter looked up
after inserting her arms into the sleeves of her winter coat,
and in a dreamy voice that seemed to come
from another world, said, *Yossi*—
her cousin, whom she hadn't spoken to or of
in over a year, who had drowned in an accident
the week before
without us telling her—
is the funniest person alive.

LONG PRAYER

In a back room off the yeshiva's large study hall—
fading wooden floors, a rabbi dreaming
at the next table—
I learn a Chassidic discourse with my cousin's son
on how Jews' commitment is greater now
than in temple times. For, now,
so many questions, such a long exile,
and still a Jew goes on.
Soon, my cousin's son will earn his rabbinic degree, get engaged,
and then drown in a scuba diving accident.

Leading the repetition of the Amida
at the shiva house,
my cousin will pause for what will seem like forever
at the end of the prayer,
Blessed is the God who resuscitates the dead.
The other worshippers won't know what to do.
I will be standing next to the bookshelf
where his son's teffilin lie unused in their case,
his name, Yossef, stitched into the cloth.
Finally, he will conclude the blessing.

Two years later, I will hold
my sister and brother-in-law's son
in a synagogue
at the top of a great hill.
He's just had his Bris and has been named
after my brother-in-law's father, who died
before he reached forty.
The Mohel is my cousin, who lost his son. The men dance
around me and the baby. I am looking down,
see my cousin's black shoes stomping the floor,
going around in a circle.

IN THE MIDDLE OF THE IN-CLASS ESSAY EXAM

I looked out at my students' faces
in the remedial classroom at the State University.

        Each mind absorbed in the quiet universe
of its respective thesis,
              each pencil rowing deeper
        into the bluebook's waters.

Yes, I thought—
        we were physical bodies
              bent over hard plastic desks,
some of us toiling at something our genes
or circumstances had made difficult for us,
              but beneath this corporeal curtain,
behind this external story of cause and effect,
           we each derived from a series of Hebrew letters,
              just mystical energy manifesting.
                        And then

the young man from Peru via Newark—
        who had graced us with his presence
but forgotten his textbook—
          stood up in his tight blue polo shirt,
              desk skittering forward,
as he belted out his announcement:
I hate my life. I'm gonna fail the class
    a second time.

He grabbed his phone and red sports drink,
              slammed the door.
Then, deeper silence:
        quiet as water, field, and sky
              the millisecond
                    that followed man's first failure.

V

SELF-PORTRAIT

Between one and five children
have crawled into your bed
at undetermined hours throughout the night.
You rise and head to the kitchen in darkness,
press the coffee button, wash your hands with the ritual cup,
say the morning blessings, drive off in a modern silver car.

Before morning prayers,
with an accountant,
you study the Chassidic text that claims
God's concealment in this world
is not real,
but more like a lofty idea enclothed in a parable
for a simple audience.
God is present just the same
within the finite world. After prayers,

a truck with spiked wheels drifts
into your lane, and you forget what you learned
the previous hour, envision your children
growing up without you,
wife marrying another man.
In a basement office with no windows, a student—
tarantula tattoo climbing down his forearm—
hands you a poem about the things his girlfriend did
with his friend on spring vacation
and asks for suggestions
because he is a deep believer.
You forget you wear a Chassidic beard,
think of yourself, still, as a young man
in a college cafeteria, trying to get the dark-haired stranger
a table away
to look back at you.

In the silver car once more, you listen
to a recorded lecture that claims
God's unseeable Essence is most present
in this lowly realm. You notice the absence
of your E-Z Pass tag as you near the bridge,
reach under your seat, consider a million possible stories
of concealment, find it in the glove compartment
just as you enter the tollbooth.

The lecture goes on in the background:
In this world, God is just hiding from Himself.
On the Bay Parkway, Chassidic men
walk along the water with their wives.
The sky is orange and red. You think of your own wife
cutting cucumbers for your lunch.
You should thank her, stop off and buy something,
but you'd be late.

The elevator is broken again in the building
the Jewish night college rents from the high school.
Out of breath, you enter the classroom—
walls covered with pictures of Spanish teachers
in sombreros—
to teach poetry to seminary students
in long dark skirts. They are not sure
what to make of you
or their lives. But when you discuss the famous poem
about a father who rises early each morning
to heat the frozen house, one begins to cry.

This morning, the discourse said everything
in this world mirrors and stems from
its spiritual source above,
like signifier linking back to signified.
What does the race through the streets
to beat the men to the bridge
where they work all night
represent? You park the car,
walk up the dark pathway to your front door.
There is light in one window.

GLOSSARY

Amida: A long prayer recited quietly by each worshiper and then repeated, out loud, by the prayer leader. One of the blessings in the Amida praises God for resuscitating the dead—a reference to the Messianic Era, when, according to Jewish tradition, those who have passed away will be brought back to life.

Aleph-Beis: The Hebrew alphabet.

Bima: The lectern or table on which the Torah is placed during communal Torah readings.

Bris: Hebrew for covenant, the term refers to a Jewish ritual circumcision. Ideally, a circumcision is performed when a boy is eight days old.

Chassidim: Hebrew, plural form of Chassid or Hasid.

Cheder: A traditional, Jewish elementary school.

Mohel: An individual trained to perform ritual circumcisions.

Mordechai: A Jewish leader during the Babylonian Exile, one of the heroes of the Purim story. Though, at the time, many Jews exiled to Persia had assimilated and given up hope of returning to Jerusalem, Mordechai inspired these Jews to reclaim their Jewish identity and traditions.

Pesach: Hebrew for Passover, the Biblical holiday commemorating the Jewish people's redemption from Egyptian slavery.

Purim: A rabbinic holiday commemorating the miraculous salvation of the Jewish people during the Babylonian Exile. Because, on the surface, salvation in the Purim story appears to have resulted from a series of coincidences—miracles disguised in nature—it's customary to dress up, to disguise oneself, on this holiday.

Rabbi/Rebbe: A Rebbe is a Jewish mystic and holy man, the leader of a Chassidic group made up of Chassids, or, in Hebrew, Chassidim. In contrast, Rabbi is a title assigned to anyone who has received rabbinical ordination.

Shiva House: Shiva is Hebrew for seven. During the first seven days of the mourning process, one who has lost a close relative remains in his or her home, where the daily prayer services are conducted and friends and family come to offer comfort.

Shul: Yiddish for synagogue.

Sukkos: A Biblical holiday commemorating the protection and shelter God provided for the Jewish people after freeing them from Egyptian slavery. Much of the holiday is spent in temporary outdoor booths. The intermediate days of the holiday are marked by special celebration, dancing, and music.

Teffilin: Hebrew for Phylacteries, Teffilin consist of two leather boxes containing sacred Biblical passages. Traditionally, Teffilin are worn on the head and bicep (near the heart), reminding the worshipper to dedicate mind and heart to God.

Yaakov and ***Aisav***: Hebrew for Jacob and Esau, Biblical twins whose rivalry is narrated in *Genesis*, where Jacob disguises himself in Esau's garments to secure his older brother's birthright.

NOTES ON POEMS

"Two Worlds Exist"

The beginning of section III refers to a mystical teaching cited and explained in Chapter 26 of *Tanya*, a Chassidic work authored by the Alter Rebbe, Rabbi Schneur Zalman of Liadi.

"The Life of Body and Soul"

The barren woman referenced in the poem is Chanah, whose confrontation with Eli, the High Priest at the time, is recorded in *Samuel I*. A number of the traditions surrounding Jewish prayer derive from Chanah's method of supplication while in the Sanctuary at Shiloh. The poem also borrows from an interpretation of the Chanah episode that appears in the Lubavitcher Rebbe's *Likkutei Sichos*, Volume 19, pages 291-297.

"The Lower Realm"

Section II: The Maggid of Mezrich, Rabbi DovBer, taught that the ten Divine utterances associated with the creation narrative in *Genesis* correspond to the Ten Commandments.

In his book of interwoven Chassidic discourses, *Yom Tov Shel Rosh Hashanah 5666*, the Rebbe Rashab, Rabbi Shalom Dovber Schneerson, suggests that this physical world—as opposed to the higher spiritual realms—is the stage on which the ultimate purpose of creation plays out. If this were not so, he reasons, God could have concluded creation by merely constructing the upper worlds that precede this physical reality.

Section III: "The beginning is wedged in the end" is a teaching that first appears in *Sefer Yetzira*, an ancient work of Jewish mysticism.

ABOUT THE AUTHOR

Yehoshua November's first poetry collection, *God's Optimism*, won the Main Street Rag Poetry Book Award and was a finalist for the *LA Times* Book Prize. November's poems have appeared in *Prairie Schooner*, *The Sun*, *Virginia Quarterly Review*, and *The Writer's Almanac*. He teaches at Rutgers University and Touro College and lives in Teaneck, NJ, with his wife and children.

ABOUT ORISON BOOKS

Orison Books is a 501(c)3 non-profit literary press focused on the life of the spirit from a broad and inclusive range of perspectives. We seek to publish books of exceptional poetry, fiction, and non-fiction from perspectives spanning the spectrum of spiritual and religious thought, ethnicity, gender identity, and sexual orientation.

As a non-profit literary press, Orison Books depends on the support of donors. To find out more about our mission and our books, or to make a donation, please visit www.orisonbooks.com.